THOUGHTS OF LOVE

RONALD E. HOLTMAN

ILLUSTRATIONS

SELA WHITNEY

DEDICATION

For Prue

I love how you engage your day in peaceful industry,

how you tend your lush gardens
or clatter gently in your kitchen.

I love the sound of spices grinding in their mill,
the smell of bread baking,

the notes to your grandchildren,

needles clicking toward mittens,

the soft turning of pages.

I love the depth of your tranquility,
those clear fathoms that, from deep within,
resound back the echoes of your affection.

I love your tenderness, your gentle touch,
and how your quiet serenity
peals out the song of our life together.

Contents

I

Gliding on lilies
Their pads slip under the hull
Shushing my canoe

One Way to Start Your Day

Rise before dawn,
light the wood stove,
brew the coffee and,

in the rich aroma,
feel the kindling's crackle.
Read something

spiritual or poetic,
maybe Gomes or Kooser,
Gorman or Whyte.

Watch the morning
steal in
through the dark trees.

Listen for the day's first chirp.

SILENCE

This morning,
on my cedar fence,
a tiger swallowtail
slowly lifts its wrinkled wings
to dry in the gentle breeze.

Newly emergent
from its chrysalis,
it awakens tentatively,
tiptoeing
into its strange new world.

Together, we stay awhile,
as the tiger pulses,
then basks,
pulses,
then basks again.

Finally, with dry wings,
it lifts off
in palpable silence,
flashing its black and yellow
against the woods' fresh green.

SUET FEEDER

Like nervous commuters
holding tickets for the next train,
downy woodpeckers pace
up and down the ash tree.

Communal but not friendly,
cautiously patient,
they fidget for their place
until the feeder clears and they hop on.

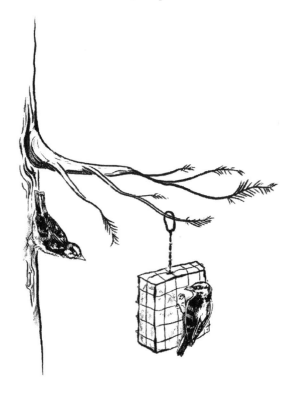

SPRING

Barren maples clack
Wendigo's bony rattle
Winter's final plaint

Barn Swallows

Each night at dusk, they come:
chattering charioteers
racing 'round the house.

Their nest tidied,
fledglings fed,
they fly off in mad pursuit.

Parents' night out.

SUNSET

For an instant just before sundown,
the dropping light paints
an orange band above the horizon,
separating the blue from its darker land.

Against that band of color,
the trees become black silhouettes,
like shadow puppets
on a lighted sheet.

Nephila, Golden Orb Weaver

"I love the colorful clothes she wears and the way the sunlight plays upon her hair."

—the Beach Boys, "Good Vibrations"

By her snare, an intricate embroidery,
she waits, masked over yellow tights,
bare legs in black leather boots.

Her lover steps onto the web's edge,
and she feels the music in his walk,
the good vibrations

as he approaches her lair.

WIND PUMP

When built,
its blades and vane
stood twenty feet,
a flash of geometry
for everyone to see.

But later,
save the axle's squeak,
it disappeared,
obscured
by familiarity.

And when electric
finally hushed its drone,
recasting it as
a prairie sundial,

there on the vane's arm
we saw a redtail hawk

perched, waiting,

to lift from that old spire
and plunge earthward toward its prey.

II

Amid Queen Anne's lace
Cornflower-blue pennants wave
A royal greeting

COMMUNION

If you have seen the strongest trees
sway gently in a silent wind,
heard a barred owl call in the night,
watched lightning pulse from cloud to cloud,

then you'll know how a
small crust of bread could nourish a
body, show friendship, or honor
sacrifice, and you would believe

that promises might flow in wine
the way each dawn rises out of
darkness, or how cascading love
replenishes pardon's deep pool,

and be assured that no matter
what languishes from your parting,
you will always remember when
you gathered to share that last meal.

TENDING

It's the simple things:
the way she kneads her dough,
then peels the round loaves
onto a hot stone,

how he splits the wood,
then stacks it in long rows,
finished with pillars
to keep the cords intact.

Tasks done with pride of craft,
best appreciated
when the fire warms,
the bread is served.

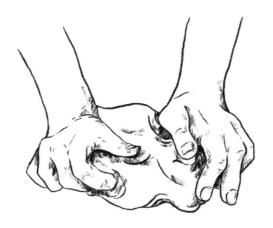

HUSBAND

From her kitchen window, she watches him
crossing the field, measuring the harvest.
She smiles at how he's carved
their names into this hardscrabble land.

Before they met, she dreamed
of patent pumps in rainbow colors,
elegant receptions at the club,
black silk and pearls at the symphony.

Then she startled her parents
by returning to their manicured lawns
with a boy whose pickup truck
resembled their gardener's wheels.

She heard a litany of fears spoken then,
the plaintive arguments for reason
and good sense, to share a life of comfort
sheltered from the prairie winds.

But he fits her like an old work shoe,
tracking in, underfoot, crowding the hall,
yet comfortable in a way that belies
the scars from stubborn rocks and shovel points.

Hearing him climb the back porch steps,
she meets him inside the screen door
and inhales the cool fall air
still clinging to his wool shirt.

Pausing in the aromas of her oven,
they watch a circling hawk
and let a red sun slip behind the barn.
Dinner's ready, she says.

THOUGHTS OF LOVE

Love's secret, she said,
is a bed too small for two
side by side. She meant
that one log cannot burn alone.

It needs the smoldering embrace of another's warmth,
the silent flickering of red and orange,
the blazing toward white-hot embers,

the pure grey ash.

~*~

In the shade of a maple tree
near the community food pantry,
a man sits on a wall,
savoring a generous sandwich.

He drops crumbs to a begging pigeon.

His belongings
impede the sidewalk,
so pedestrians steer around,
crossing over the tree lawn,

but one man stops,
and as they chat,
crimson leaves
drift down around them.

~*~

In the thicket of the deepest wood,
where fallen cedars
tangle in a faceless maze,

a forester, tools in hand,
studies that forbidding place,
sees how shafts of light reveal

a fern or lichen on a granite face.
He clears the deadfall, and
when a path is found,

the glade discerned,
he rests against a stump,
emersed in all the shades of green.

~*~

By the granite wall,
she births from fallow ground

columbine and yarrow,
lavender and coral bells.

She tends them patiently,
plucking out the obstinance,

and all of nature beats its wings
to sip the fragrance there.

FOR PAT

When the door closed and
all you had was silence,
some plain walls,
and a simple bed,

when a crust of bread,
your daily prayers,
and sepia dreams
were your only comforts,

somehow you kept the fire
smoldering in your heart,
cradling the ember safely
like an ancient fire-bearer

until that new shining day
when the door opened again
and the fresh air
awakened the flames.

You had learned by then
how courage and determination,
with God's grace,
had saved you.

And so many times after,
you lavished your warmth
on others who, like you,
had felt the chill

of loneliness or despair.
And in all things difficult,
you have shown us
how to always tend the fire.

FOR DAVID

When we see a distant shore to explore,

> a mountain path to climb,
> a meandering river to paddle,
> a fire ring needing flames for warmth,
> a slope of powder whispering for skis, or
> winding asphalt yearning the song of rolling wheels,

We'll think of you and how you did it all.

And when the young among us ask about the wilderness,

> where a trail beckons to rocky heights and broad vistas,
> a hungry bass leaps to take the lure,
> a loon calls across a northern lake,
> an eagle lifts from its high perch and soars aloft,
> or where the setting sun blazes orange across still waters,

We'll think of you and how you led other youth like them to see those things.

And when friends and family gather for love and consolation,

> over a cup of coffee,
> a crystal glass of wine,
> a sumptuous meal,

We'll think of how you served them all of that —and more.

And if we're still wanting solace,

> there will always be
> the robust aroma
> of a fine cigar.

Bon voyage, my friend. Safe travels.

For J. C.

"After a while nothing exists of the world but thoughts about
fly fishing."

—Norman Maclean, *A River Runs Through It*

I'll think of you wading
the Yellowstone upstream,
into a brace of cool Rockies air.

A golden Big Sky morning
glints off the riffles
before the fast water.

The fly on your tippet
matches the morning hatch
you've seen swarming there.

You're stalking the wary Brown
lurking in the bank undercut
at the edge of the rapids.

The arc of your rod,
sweeps between 10 and 2
in a graceful four count,

looping the line out,
then settling the fly
over the dark water.

I'll think of the thrill
at the splash and swirl
just before you set the hook

and how, with one hand,
you'll net the trout.
As a gesture of thanks,

you'll return it to the river,
a sportsman's courtesy
toward a worthy opponent.

Fence-Sitters

He's not more than four,
all straw hat and overalls.
He straddles the top
of the wooden pasture gate

while his sister, maybe ten,
mows the ground
by her roadside stand.

Cut grass sticks to her bare legs.

Her baskets brim with pole beans,
peppers, melons, and tomatoes.

When her tasks are finished,
she flips the sign to "Open,"
then joins her brother on the fence.

Together, they listen for the rush of passing cars.

III

Lumberjack chainsaws
Sing through virgin forest stands
Cedars take their bows

Spitfire

It came in a box,
full of thin sheets of balsa,
a fold of tissue paper,
a long rubber band,
and a plastic propeller.

On an old card table,
with a razor-sharp knife,
I cut out the pieces,
glued them into a skeleton,
covered it with the tissue.

I still remember
how the tissue dried taut
after a spritz of water,
the way a coating of dope
toughened the skin,

how a pinch of clay would
level its glide path,
how it would leap from my hand
to fly across the yard,
landing softly in the grass.

But I can't explain how,
after construction, I found
one stray part of the fuselage,
somehow left on the table
under the box.

LAUNDRESS

From early morning until dusk,
the bundles arrive, confessing.

She clutches them to her breast,
embracing their venial sins:
this one's smoking habit,
a collar's lipstick stain,
the musk of cheap cologne.

She takes them all without judgment,
promising only their return, clean and reborn.

RAGMAN

Rags! he called from his wagon
as it creaked down our street.
We'd feed his mare our carrot tops,
compost to us but lifeblood to her.
We gave him our discards,
not worth saving, too good to throw away.
He piled them precariously on top,
then rumbled on.

I wonder now about that old man,
his wagon, and his horse.
At eventide, did his children run to him,
their mama in the doorway, apron-clad?
Did he retire, or was he pushed aside
by garbage trucks and union suits?
At his death did they write
of how he lived on rags and trash?

Did he ever walk a mountain trail
and stop to wonder at the view?

SLEDDING

The boys lead, cutting the trail,
lifting their legs high,
then setting them down,
a half-time marching band.

The father walks behind,
towing a red plastic sled.
They are resolute,
parading to the crest,
where they wait
for the run to clear.

The youngest one
dips his mitten in snow,
touches the crystals
to his tongue.

Then they climb on,
stacked in tight,
and fly downhill,
laughing into the powder.

Sound Check at the Stanford Memorial Church

Avoiding the rain, we ducked into the open sanctuary,
the silence broken only by whispers from the corners:

... ready ... ready ... ready ... ready ....

And then from the sound board, Alicia Keys sang,

So every time you hold me,
-check-

Every time you kiss me,
  -check-

Every time you touch me,
    -check-

Promise that you'll love me.[1]
      -check-

Above us, a cloud moved, and sunlight streamed through the
stained glass.

---

[1] Alicia Keys, "Like You'll Never See Me Again," *As I Am*, Lellow
Productions/EMI Music Publishing, Inc.

CHILDREN

"Let the children come to me . . . for to such belongs the
kingdom of Heaven."

—Luke 19:14

On a Chicago winter night
where the wind ices the city,
a child sleeps in the warmth
of his mother's breast.

Or perhaps she's wrapped in a *shuka*
on some African plain, where the heat
is a blazing sun and a thousand
fires of frustration and chaos.

Both children rest peacefully,
innocent of the random drive-by,
the explosive, senseless terror
that lurks to kill the world's hope

while each mother asks herself,
could my child
grow to teach,
or heal or prophesy,

and could my child change the world?

CANOE

"There is a time of change in a wilderness trip when patterns
that have been left behind fade beneath the immediacies of
wind, sun, rain, and fire, and a different sense of distance, of
shelter, of food."

—John McPhee, The Survival of the Bark Canoe

If you've ever paddled a canoe
made of canvas
stretched over cedar strips

or better yet,
one of birch bark
from some ancient design,

you'd know how a wood canoe
glides straight and silent
over the mirrors of blue water.

I now use one molded
from Kevlar, a pliable synthetic
nearly weightless, maintenance free.

But I'm annoyed by the drift
of its rounded hull and I
pine for the old days,

until the first portage.

STRANGERS IN MONTANA

When we walked into that small-town bar,
the stools swiveled in concert, asking,
Where you boys from?

They already knew of our leisure,
paddling canoes down the Missouri
while they threshed miles of summer wheat.

Together, we occupied that smoky space,
nursing longnecks in unspoken tension,
an atmosphere where sparks could fly.

Then Tony approached their end of the bar.
Say, he asked, *any of you fellas own a Sharps?*

And it turned out that one of the cowboys
knew another, who knew a man
who made replicas of that famous rifle.

And the locals bought the next round.

GIVING UP THE FARM

For Frank and Lenora

From a leather chair,
over wire-rimmed glasses,
the banker told you,
It's nothing personal,
just no way
you can pay the loan.

You already knew it
from the red ledger
you left at home,
sprawled open
on the painted
kitchen table.

But still, leaving the bank
for your battered truck,
where she waited,
hands clasped,

you fretted saying,
Reckon we're done.

You're a good man, she replied.
We'll make do.

With no spring plowing,
you stowed the gear,
left the animals to forage,
and gleaned coal
spilled along the tracks.

Then you went out to look for work.

ALONE

I last saw him
walking a road
to nowhere in particular,
as if he had all day
to get there.

By then his mother
was long gone
and all he had left
was his birthmark and
a disabled gait.

He accompanied her everywhere.
If she had some meeting to attend,
he waited patiently
for their long walk home.

As she lay dying,
I'm sure it broke her heart,
knowing there was no one left
to care for him,

and I can't imagine his sorrow,
learning that her last journey
was the one time
he couldn't go along.

MOURNING

At dawn, an Amishman
drives toward Benton,
past fields of shocked corn
pale with last night's frost.

Like a steam locomotive,
his mare pulses
bursts of hot breath,
enshrouding the buggy.

Headlights flash, and the
man flinches,
recalling his young bride,
their babe in her arms.

God's will, he is reminded,
but clenching the reins
will not carry him past

the skidding tires,
the splintering crash,

that on one dark night cleft his family tree
quicker than a plain man,

with but a few strokes of a well-honed ax,
could split a log of sturdy ash.

IV

TP from the field

Save paper, recycle cobs

Skip the Costco line

POLESTAR

Slaves running north toward freedom.
Portuguese sailors from their crow's nests.
Blackfeet on their painted ponies.

All discerned Ursa Major's
seven stars, the Big Dipper's
ladle edge aimed at Polaris.

Mysteriously aligned
with the axis of our world,
more reliable than a compass,

it's unquestionably been
our guiding light forever.
Yet somehow,

we still can't find our way.

GRIZZLY

A grizzly rambles down the hillside,
trampling penstemon and goldenrod,
as she canters toward the village dump.

She ignores the rhythm of our gondola
as we press our cameras on the plexiglass
to capture all the wilderness.

Once, she savored sweet meadow berries,
paws of wild honey,
fresh salmon slapped
from a spawning stream.

Now she'll hunker in the trash
to puncture soda cans
and tear the cellophane
from candy bars and spoiled meat.

At the peak's Ski Haus, we purchase
a soapstone carving of her kin,
reared back on hind legs, fangs bared,
guarding with pride the day's fresh kill.

Ecology

This mountain face,
thrust up by shifting plates,
once primordial, indestructible,
convulses now from dynamite.

Orange Cats paw the litter,
pan scraping and bulldozing
the rubbled harvest
to shape a world-class ski slope.

On a hiking trail, overlooking the work, a sign reads:
Hikers!
Stay on the path.
Help us save this fragile scene.

GREEN MOUNTAIN MIDDEN

This wilderness trail
in the Green Mountains
is littered

as if

John Chapman's evil twin
gave up on apples
and sowed trash instead.

In his wake, sunlight refracts rainbows
through new-age water bottles.

Copper ferns unfurl in brown glass shards.

Bloodroot blossoms from white milk jugs.

Maples shine like soda cans, stacked against the sky.

Where are the scavengers,
those barefoot children
who could harvest these?

The plastic could be filled,
the glass affixed on privacy walls,
the cans smoothed into roof shingles.

Ingenious ones could live
on the fruit of these empties,
this endless bounty of affluence.

CRYPTOCURRENCY

Think of a washerwoman
bent over her tub, scrubbing
the Emperor's new clothes,
her mouth full of clothespins.

His Highness
pays her in greenbacks,
assured by the magic
of her laundering.

The neighbors see only
his bare bottom line.

His multihued trade balance
rises like a soap bubble, then
pops silently in the breeze.

THE STATE OF THE UNION

"He [the President] shall from time to time give to the Congress information of the state of the union and recommend to their consideration such measures as he shall judge necessary and expedient;…"

—United States Constitution, Article II, Section 3, Clause 1

It's become the Superbowl of politics
wrapped in
pregame analysis,
wardrobe malfunctions,
smoke and mirrors,
grand entrances,
talking heads,
instant replay,
cheering and booing,
endless commercials,
postgame analysis.

A cacophony of everyone talking at once, and no one listening.

Joshua Wong's Light

"I lift my lamp beside the golden door."

—Emma Lazarus, "The New Colossus"

On a rainy day in Hong Kong,
on the other side of the world,
a young man in a white T-shirt
asks the gathered masses
to raise their cell phones for freedom.

And in the Great Hall of the People,
where the power is generated,
the doctrines scribed,
the schemes plotted,
the cells filled,

the ideologues will someday learn
that there is no brighter light
than the one shining at the door
to welcome the traveler
emerging from darkness.

CUSTOMER SERVICE

Hello, welcome to America. Hablas español? Por favor responde sí o no.

This call may be monitored for quality assurance.

If you are calling from a touch-tone phone and know the extension of the person you wish to reach, please dial that extension now. Otherwise, please listen to the following prompts, as they have changed.

If you are seeking political asylum, please press 1.

If you want to sell cheap goods made by child labor, please press 2.

If you are inquiring about a drug delivery, please press 3.

If you wish to impose your religious or political views by violent means, please press 4.

If you wish to increase your wealth through fraud or deception, please press 5.

If you wish to make a political campaign contribution or influence our elections, please press 6.

If you just want to live here with the huddled masses yearning to breathe free, please hold and a slum landlord will come on the line to assist you.

The Bully

Luke, a shy kid in my third grade, sat aloof.
Plainly dressed, uncoiffed,
his passivity escaped us.

He never explained himself, just hunkered
over his desk, mystified by i before e,
carrying the 1 in multiplication.

His thick pencil was a soft graphite.
Erasures smudged his work
or sometimes tore his lined paper.

Once, I asked him why he would eat
the blackened banana from his lunch pail.
He merely shrugged.

Bear, a big brash kid,
a sluggard at his desk,
had grand designs for ruling the class.

Bear asserted himself
by imposing random pain.
He chose his victims wisely:

not the wiry kid who'd go for the groin,
nor the one who would squeal for relief.
Instead, Bear chose the pacifist, Luke.

Bear pestered and shoved him,
dislodged him from the lunch line,
announcing each assault as justice

for someone who wouldn't defend himself.
I could blacken Luke's eye, Bear said,
and I'll do it if he don't watch out.

By fourth grade, Luke was gone,
and we knew that Bear would choose again,
because not one of us had stood up for Luke.

RAVEN

"It's nearly over now. Most of the villages are abandoned, and those which have not entirely vanished lie in ruins. . . .Perhaps it's time the Raven started looking for another clamshell."

—Haida myth, as told by Bill Reid

In an outdoor restaurant
overlooking Vancouver's harbor,
a raven alights above the diners,
squawking.

He craps a white splash
on the teak floor,
then drops to the aisle
to wander under the tables.

He's a black-robed prophet
from the wilderness,
disrupting conversations,
amusing some, distressing others,

all the while preaching

at the elegance of diners
hunched over white tablecloths,
the gourmet food on fine china,
crystal glasses of wine.

He relishes the table scraps
as if the crumbs of
civilization's affluence
could be his savory locusts,
even honey.

COVID

We're exhausted, deflated,

like that blowup Santa,
now a red-and-white heap
crumpled over the dirty snow
on your neighbor's front lawn.

Masks on, masks off,
work from home or away,
we're riptorn and confused
by the relentless jabs

of self-interest,
claims of independence,
the lure of home remedies,
the witchery of stubbornness.

Flattened, limp,
we are all gasping for air.

ACKNOWLEDGEMENTS

Thanks to my friends Anthony, Maryanna and Frank (Gus) Biggio, Sara Patton, Emily Hershberger and David Wilcox for their reviews and suggestions.

Thanks to David and Elsie Kline for publishing "Husband" in Farming Magazine.

Thanks to the following persons for giving me permission to use their poems: Patricia Herbold – "For Pat;" Carol Briggs – "For David;" and Gennie Johnston - "For J.C."

Thanks also to my editors Angela B. Wade and Amanda Vacharat.

Finally, thanks to Sela Whitney for her illustrations and cover design.

The author is a graduate of Denison University and Case Western Reserve University Law School. Retired from his law practice, he lives in rural Ohio. His first book of poetry, **Limit Theory**, was published in 2013.

Sela Whitney is a current student at Columbus College of Art & Design. Her artistic interests range from illustration to graphic design. You can find her on **Instagram** at **selawhitney_art** or on her website: https://selawhitney10.wixsite.com/selaart

Made in United States
Troutdale, OR
08/06/2023